OUR WORLD 5

SECOND EDITION • GRAMMAR WORKBOOK

Series Editors
Joan Kang Shin
JoAnn (Jodi) Crandall

NATIONAL GEOGRAPHIC LEARNING

Australia • Brazil • Mexico • Singapore • United Kingdom • United States

Unit 1

Future predictions and plans with *be going to*

It'**s**	**going to**	rain	tomorrow.	*It's = It is* *I'm = I am* *They're = They are*
I'**m**		call	my friend.	
They'**re**		play	basketball.	

Question						**Answer**
	Is	it	**going to**	rain	tomorrow?	Yes, it is. No, it isn't.
What	**are**	they		do		They'**re going to** play basketball.

Use *be going to* to talk about the future.

1 **Read.** Complete the sentences.

1. We just saw lightning. Next there _'s going to_ be thunder.
2. A sandstorm is coming. My parents ________ get the house ready.
3. It's snowing. He ________ wear a warm coat.
4. It's hot today. I ________ go swimming.

2 **Read and write.** Answer the questions. Use *going to* and phrases from the box.

bring an umbrella close all the windows evacuate ~~make a snowman~~

1. What are you going to do in the snow?
   I'm going to make a snowman.
2. What are you going to do if it's rainy?
   ____
3. How is your family going to get ready for the sandstorm?
   ____
4. What are your cousins going to do if there's a flood?
   ____

3 **Read and write.** Read about what's happening today. Then say that tomorrow things are going to be different.

1. Today it's really cold.

   Tomorrow it's going to be hot.

2. Today I'm getting up early.

   ____

3. Today my brother is staying home.

   ____

4. Today my parents aren't working.

   ____

5. Today it's raining.

   ____

4 **Read and write.** Answer with information that is true for you.

1. Is it going to rain much this week where you live?

   No, but it's going to be cloudy.

2. What are you <u>not</u> going to do if there's thunder and lightning?

   ____

3. What are you going to do if there's a flood?

   ____

4. If you have to evacuate your house, where are you going to go?

   ____

5 **Write.** There's no school because of a blizzard. Write four things you're going to do today.

____

____

____

____

Zero conditional (present tense)

If	it	**snows,**		school	**starts**	late.
	it	**is**	raining,	I	**use**	an umbrella.
	I	**go to bed**	late,	I	**am**	tired the next day.

These two sentences mean the same thing. In sentence 1, notice the comma.
If it snows, school starts late.
School starts late if it snows.

1 **Read.** Circle the correct answer.

1. **If there** / **There's** is an emergency, we follow our plan.
2. If it rains, then **if I use** / **I use** an umbrella.
3. If a tornado comes, **if we evacuate** / **we evacuate**.
4. If Jon knows it's going to be cold, he **wears** / **wore** his coat and gloves.
5. **Is** / **If** it's hot, we go swimming.
6. If **there** / **there's** a blizzard, we don't have school.

2 **Read and write.** Complete the sentences.

1. If it's hurricane season, it rains a lot.
2. If it snows, ______________________
3. If the electricity goes out, ______________________
4. If a blizzard comes, ______________________
5. If there's no rain for weeks, ______________________
6. If there's a flood in my town, ______________________

3 **Read and write.** Complete the sentences with a phrase beginning with *if*.

1. If there's a blizzard ______, people can't drive.
2. ______, we need a flashlight.
3. ______, I make an emergency plan.
4. ______, I call my parents.
5. ______, people evacuate.
6. ______, we go to a storm shelter.

4 **Read and write.** Answer the questions in complete sentences.

1. What do people wear if it rains?

   If it rains, people wear rain boots.
2. What do you do if it snows?

   ______
3. What does your family do if a tornado comes?

   ______
4. What do dogs do if there is a heat wave?

   ______

5 **Write.** Write five sentences using the phrases in the box and *if*.

be very windy	feel cold	hear about a tornado on the radio
miss the bus	~~see a lion~~	see thunder and lightning

If I see a lion, I run.

______

______

______

______

Unit 2

Comparisons with *as . . . as*

The frog	is	**as**	big	**as**	my hand.
Lions	are**n't**		fast		cheetahs.

as . . . as = The two things are the same.
not as . . . as = The two things are different.

1 **Read.** Circle the correct answer.

1. A cheetah is **faster than** / **as fast as** an elephant.
2. An elephant is **larger than** / **as large as** a horse.
3. A poisonous spider is **more dangerous than** / **as dangerous as** a non-poisonous spider.
4. Zebras are about **as big as** / **much bigger than** horses.
5. A bee is **smaller than** / **as small as** a salamander.

2 **Read and write.** Compare using *as . . . as* and the words in parentheses.

1. A deer is not ____________ (fast) a jaguar.
2. Otters can be ____________ (playful) monkeys.
3. Some frogs are ____________ (poisonous) snakes.
4. Donkeys are not ____________ (beautiful) horses.
5. An elephant is not ____________ (loud) a lion.
6. An alligator's skin is not ____________ (smooth) a seal's skin.

3 **Read and write.** Compare using *(not) as . . . as.*

1. A bee's sting can be dangerous, but a poisonous spider's bite is more dangerous!

   A bee's sting is not as dangerous as a poisonous spider's bite.

2. My sister thinks baby seals are really cute. She thinks lion cubs are really cute, too!

   ____

3. Cheetahs can run at a speed of around 110 kph (68 mph). Sailfish can swim 110 kph.

   ____

4. A baby elephant is big! It weighs about 90 kg (200 lb.), the same as two small people.

   ____

4 **Write.** Compare using *(not) as . . . as.*

1. insect / leaf

   Some insects are as green as a leaf.

2. cat's fur / rabbit's fur

   ____

3. seal / elephant

   ____

4. snakes / crocodiles

   ____

5. baby seal / baby otter

   ____

5 **Write.** Write five sentences comparing yourself to people just like you.

I am as old as my cousin Jack.

____

____

____

____

Tag questions

Positive			Negative	
The tiger	**is**	beautiful,	**isn't**	it?
Rabbits	**are**	fast,	**aren't**	they?
The lion	**was**	loud,	**wasn't**	it?
Dinosaurs	**were**	everywhere,	**weren't**	they?
You	**eat**	bread,	**don't**	you?
A spider	**eats**	insects,	**doesn't**	it?
The turtles	**ate**	the fish,	**didn't**	they?

Negative			Positive	
This snake	**isn't**	poisonous,	**is**	it?
You	**aren't**	afraid of bees,	**are**	you?
That fish	**wasn't**	dangerous,	**was**	it?
Those	**weren't**	ants,	**were**	they?
You	**don't** eat	bread,	**do**	you?
A spider	**doesn't** eat	plants,	**does**	it?
The turtles	**didn't** eat	the fish,	**did**	they?

Use a pronoun at the end of the sentence.
The tiger is beautiful, isn't it?
Rabbits are fast, aren't they?

1 **Read.** Circle the letter.

1. Some species look like others, ______?
   a. do they b. don't they c. aren't they
2. Copycat animals are amazing, ______?
   a. isn't they b. don't they c. aren't they
3. Those deer weren't running from a lion, ______?
   a. were they b. aren't they c. weren't they
4. Donkeys are funny animals, ______?
   a. can't they b. aren't they c. are they

2 **Read and write.** Complete the questions.

1. Some insects are poisonous, ________________?
2. Camouflage doesn't help all animals hide, ________________?
3. Those fish swim fast, ________________?
4. That frog had stripes, ________________?
5. A cheetah can run faster than a human, ________________?
6. The dog we saw yesterday wasn't very nice, ________________?

3 **Look and write.** Ask a question about each animal.

1.  This butterfly is beautiful, isn't it? ____________________

2.  ____________________

3.  ____________________

4.  ____________________

5.  ____________________

6.  ____________________

4 **Write.** Write four questions to ask your friend about this week's events.

The game we played after school was fun, wasn't it?

____

____

____

____

Unit 3

Present perfect with *ever* and *never*

<table>
<tr><th colspan="5">Question</th><th>Answer</th><th></th></tr>
<tr><td rowspan="2">Have</td><td rowspan="2">you</td><td rowspan="4">ever</td><td rowspan="2">played</td><td rowspan="2">the drums?</td><td>Yes, I have.
Yes, I’ve played them many times.</td><td rowspan="2">I’ve = I have
haven’t = have not</td></tr>
<tr><td>No, I haven’t.
No, I’ve <u>never</u> played the drums.</td></tr>
<tr><td rowspan="2">Has</td><td rowspan="2">he</td><td rowspan="2">heard</td><td rowspan="2">that song?</td><td>Yes, he has.
Yes, he’s heard that song twice.</td><td rowspan="2">he’s = he has
hasn’t = has not</td></tr>
<tr><td>No, he hasn’t.
No, he’s <u>never</u> heard that song.</td></tr>
</table>

twice = two times
never = at no time in the past

1 **Read and match.** Draw a line.

1. Has she ever sung in a band?
2. Have you ever danced at a concert?
3. Have they ever played music together?
4. Has he seen his favorite band play?
5. Have we ever been in band class together?

a. No, I never have.
b. Yes, she has.
c. No, we never have.
d. Yes, they have.
e. No, he never has.

2 **Read.** Complete the sentences with *ever* or *never*.

1. I have ____never____ played this instrument before.
2. I have ________________ seen your violin before.
3. This will be the first time I have ________________ played that song.
4. Have you ________________ been in an orchestra?
5. My parents have ________________ heard this band play.
6. I have ________________ felt both so nervous and so excited before.
7. Have you ________________ seen such unusual instruments?
8. No, we ________________ have.

3 **Read and write.** Answer the questions in complete sentences.

1. Have you ever played the saxophone?

   No, I have never played the saxophone.

2. Have you ever had guitar lessons?

   ____

3. Have you ever written a song?

   ____

4. Have your friends ever heard you sing?

   ____

5. Have you ever met a famous musician? If so, who?

   ____

4 **Write.** Write questions with the words. Then answer them in complete sentences.

1. flute

   Have you ever played flute?

   Yes, I have played the flute.

2. drums

   ____

   ____

3. concert

   ____

   ____

4. lead singer

   ____

   ____

5 **Write.** Write two interesting things you have done. Write two things you have never done.

I have seen a Chinese opera.

____

____

Comparative adverbs

She	sleeps	**longer**	**than**		I do.
	plays	**better**			
He	sings	**more**	**beautifully**	**than**	
	practices		**often**		

She	sleeps	**as**	**long**	**as**	I do.
	plays		**well**		
He	sings		**beautifully**		
	practices		**often**		

Irregular forms: *well* ⟶ *better (than)*   *badly* ⟶ *worse (than)*
With *often*, you can use *more* or *less*: *He practices* *<u>more often</u>* / *<u>less often</u> than I do.*

1 **Read.** Circle the correct answer.

1. I like pop music **more well** / **better** than I like rock.
2. He can't sing very well. He sings **worse** / **less better** than I do.
3. Like me, my sister practices piano every day. She practices **harder** / **as hard as** I do.
4. My dad sings **more loudly** / **as loudly** than anyone else in the family.
5. When he dances, his feet move **faster than** / **less fast** mine.
6. She plays piano on Sundays, but I play every day. She plays **better** / **less often** than I do.

2 **Write.** Complete the sentences.

1. I like being in the jazz band ___as well as___ (=, well) being in the orchestra.
2. She can play the violin ______________ (+, well) she can play the piano.
3. He listens to classical music ______________ (-, often) he listens to rock.
4. Do you sing ______________ (=, badly) your sister?
5. When my dad plays guitar, his hands move ______________ (+, fast) mine do.
6. He plays the guitar ______________ (=, often) he plays the drums.

3 **Write.** Use the words to write comparative sentences.

1. he / sing / =, well / sister

   He sings as well as his sister (does).
2. she / practice piano / -, often / brother

   ____
3. she / play flute / +, beautifully / her teacher

   ____
4. he / listen to rock music / +, often / his friend

   ____
5. musicians / play / drums / +, loudly / violin

   ____
6. I / dance ballet / =, well / hip-hop

   ____

4 **Read and write.** Answer the questions using comparatives.

1. What do you listen to more often—rock or hip-hop?

   I listen to hip-hop more often than I listen to rock.
2. Who sings better—you or your best friend?

   ____
3. What do you do as well as your parents?

   ____
4. What do you play more often—sports or music?

   ____
5. Think of your two favorite bands. Which one do you like better?

   ____

Review: Units 1–3

1 Read and match. Draw a line.

1. Is it going to snow?
2. Is it going to be warm tomorrow?
3. I see wind moving the sand.
4. A heat wave is coming.

a. If there's a sandstorm, I stay inside.
b. Yes, there's going to be a blizzard.
c. If it gets hot, I go to the pool.
d. No, it's going to be cool and windy.

2 Read and write. Complete the sentences.

1. A monkey will climb ___higher than___ (+, high) a panda, ___won't it___?
2. Some wasps are ___________ (=, poisonous) snakes, ___________?
3. An otter can swim ___________ (+, well) a dog, ___________?
4. A cheetah runs ___________ (+, fast) its prey, ___________?

3 Read and write. Complete the dialogue.

CAMILO: Have you ___________ to a sanctuary for big cats? It's like a zoo for tigers, lions, and other wild cats.

ALMA: No, I ___________.

CAMILO: Sounds cool, ___________?

ALMA: Yes, it does! Was it ___________ it sounds?

CAMILO: Even cooler! I loved all the cats. I even got to feed one of them!

ALMA: Wow! Sounds great. I'm ___________ do something cool, too. I'm ___________ see my first jazz concert! Have you ___________ to a concert?

CAMILO: Yes, ___________. My dad plays the trumpet. ___________ he has a concert, we go to see him.

4 Look and write.

1.

There's going to be a tornado.

If there's a tornado, we go to a shelter.

2.

____

____

3.

____

____

4.

____

____

5 **Write.** Respond with complete sentences.

1. Have you ever seen a cheetah? ______________________________

____

2. Compare a cheetah to another animal. ______________________________

____

3. Have you ever played an instrument? Which one? ______________________

____

4. If you're at a concert, what do you do? ______________________________

____

Unit 4

May* and *might

There	**may** **might**	(not)	be	life in our solar system outside Earth.
We			receive	messages from extraterrestrials in the future.

You can use *may* and *might* to talk about the present or the future. They mean the same thing.

1 **Read and match.** Draw a line.

1. What star is that?
2. Is there life on other planets?
3. What was that shape moving in the sky?
4. Will extraterrestrials visit Earth?

a. There might be.
b. It may be the North Star.
c. They may.
d. I thought it might be a comet.

2 **Read and write.** Complete the sentences with *may* or *might*.

1. We think Jupiter may/might have moons that we haven't discovered yet.
2. I think other solar systems ________________ also have planets like Earth.
3. Someday people ________________ be able to go to space on vacation.
4. The astronauts ________________ have to be in space for many months.
5. He ________________ go to space camp someday.
6. She didn't agree that there ________________ be life in other galaxies.
7. They knew that the big star in the sky ________________ actually be a planet.
8. Have you heard there ________________ be a new planet in our solar system?

3 **Read and write.** Use words from the box and *may* or *might.*

be	come	have	see	~~try~~	win

1. They thought extraterrestrials __might try__ to contact us.
2. Scientists say that a comet ______________ close to Earth in a few years.
3. We thought that the movie about life on other planets ______________ the prize for best film.
4. There ______________ more galaxies than we know in the universe.
5. We thought scientists ______________ water on Mars.

4 **Read and write.** Answer the questions with your own ideas. Use *may* or *might.*

1. Is there a planet that doesn't have a moon?

   There might be a planet that doesn't have a moon.
2. How long will it take to receive a message from extraterrestrials?

   ____
3. When will we next see a comet in the sky?

   ____
4. Do plants and animals live on other planets?

   ____
5. How many galaxies are there?

   ____

5 **Look and write.** Imagine this is a new planet. Write three sentences about it. Use *may* or *might.*

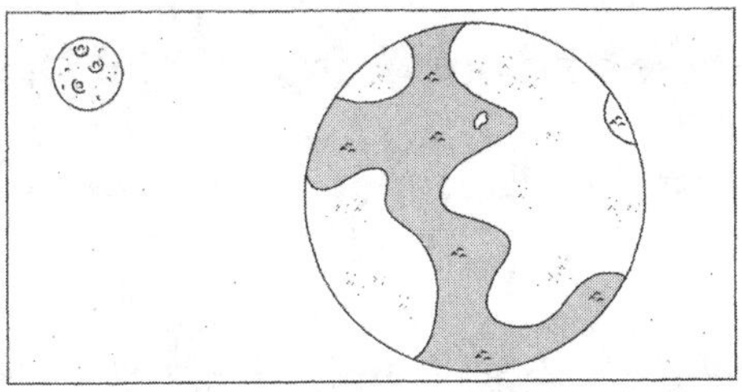

There might be trees on this planet.

____

____

____

Indefinite pronouns

Everyone in this class works hard. We all work hard.

Someone ate my apple, but I don't know who.

I don't think **anyone** wants to live on the moon.
Does **anyone** want to live on the moon?

No one was late to school yesterday. **Everyone** was on time.

Use *anyone* in negative sentences and questions.
*I don't think **anyone** wants to live on the moon.* (Not: ~~*I don't think **no one** wants to live on the moon.*~~)
*Does **anyone** want to live on the moon?* (Not: ~~*Does **someone** want to live on the moon?*~~)

1 **Read.** Match the word that can replace each underlined phrase. Draw a line.

1. Each kid in my class wants to fly to the moon.
2. Did you talk to any of the astronauts who visited school?
3. My phone is ringing. Another person is trying to call me.
4. Nobody who lives here is home.

a. no one
b. everyone
c. anyone
d. someone

2 **Read.** Circle the correct answer.

1. Outer space is really interesting! **Everyone** / **No one** is interested in space, aren't they?
2. **No one** / **Someone** from another planet might try to communicate with us. Don't be surprised if you hear about it someday.
3. Most people don't believe there's life on other planets. Does **everyone** / **anyone** think extraterrestrials are out there?
4. I want to believe in extraterrestrials, but really there's **no one** / **anyone** out there.
5. We were all invited to see the stars with a scientist. I'd like **no one** / **everyone** in the group to go.
6. **Someone** / **Anyone** is coming to speak to our class. I think it might be an astronomer.

3 **Read and write.** Complete the paragraph. Use *anyone, everyone, no one,* and *someone.*

Not ________________ says that there is life on other planets. Do you think ________________ is out there that's as smart as humans? Some people say there's ________________ out there at all. Others definitely say that there's life on other planets. Do you know ________________ who says they have seen an extraterrestrial? I want to say that ________________ is out there, but I might not really believe ________________ who said they saw an extraterrestrial.

4 **Read and write.** Rewrite the sentences. Use *anyone, everyone, no one,* and *someone.*

1. All the kids in my class went to the science center.

   Everyone went to the science center.
2. The teacher asked if any of the students knew all the planets.

   ____
3. One student could name all of them.

   ____
4. I knew that none of the students could name the comets.

   ____
5. We all learned a lot about our solar system.

   ____

5 **Look and write.** Write three questions and answers. Use *anyone, everyone, no one,* and *someone.*

Is anyone playing the violin? No, no one is playing the violin.

____

____

____

Unit 5

Gerunds as subjects

Swimming		is	good exercise.
Cooking		takes	time to learn.
Writing	stories	is	fun.
Singing	songs	brings	people together.

swim + -ing → swimming
cook + -ing → cooking
write + -ing → writing
sing + -ing → singing

1 Write. Change each word to the *-ing* form.

1. tell ________________
2. listen ________________
3. weave ________________
4. play ________________
5. create ________________
6. share ________________

2 Read and write.

1. Reading (read) my grandparents' old letters is cool.
2. ________________ (cook) with my grandmother is one of my favorite things to do.
3. ________________ (know) family traditions helps me understand my culture.
4. ________________ (share) stories is a regular activity in my family.

3 Read and write.

In my family, ________________ (keep) our culture strong over generations is very important. ________________ (cook) and ________________ (eat) traditional foods is one way my family has held on to traditions. ________________ (tell) stories is another way we share our family's history. ________________ (teach) my brothers and sisters and me about our culture is something my parents and grandparents care about. But they don't just talk—they show us what our ancestors did. For example, ________________ (make) artwork and ________________ (weave) cloth are two of our ancestors' activities that we've learned to do.

4 **Look and write.** Use the *-ing* form.

1.  ______________________ with your family is really important.

2.  ______________________ can be really fun.

3.  ______________________ is a good way to make friends.

4.  ______________________ is an important tradition in many cultures.

5 **Write.** Choose four activities or use your own. Write about your family's traditions.

cook	eat	play traditional music
read	share	~~tell stories~~
take photos	talk	visit

Storytelling is one way my family likes to pass down our history.

____

____

____

____

Gerunds as objects

I	**like**	making jewelry.
	enjoy	cooking with my grandmother.
	love	
	tried	

I'**m**	**good at**	playing	the guitar.
He'**s**	**interested in**	learning	Swahili.
We'**re**	**excited about**	visiting	the museum.
They'**re**	**tired of**	studying	for the test.

verb + *-ing* word: *I **like/enjoy/love/tried** making jewelry.*
be + **adjective** + **preposition** + *-ing* word: *I **am good at** playing the guitar.*

1 **Read and write.** Complete the sentences.

1. She likes ________________ (make) jewelry.
2. They enjoy ________________ (learn) about their family's traditions.
3. I am good at ________________ (create) handcrafted items.
4. Are you interested in ________________ (share) something about your culture?
5. My grandfather likes ________________ (tell) stories about his friends.
6. We enjoy ________________ (play) games together as a family.

2 **Unscramble.** Then circle the sentences that are true for you.

1. culture / eating / enjoy / I / foods / my / from

   I enjoy eating foods from my culture.
2. taking / I / my / family / like / pictures / of

   ____
3. fun / is / my / hands / making / things / with

   ____
4. interested / in / I'm / creating / pottery / not

   ____
5. grandma / weaving / with / is / my / fun

   ____

3 Look and write.

1.  They enjoy ________________ as a way to tell stories.

2. 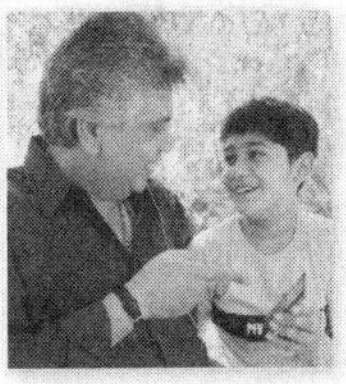 The boy is interested in ________________ music with his grandfather.

3.  She is very good at ________________ pottery.

4. 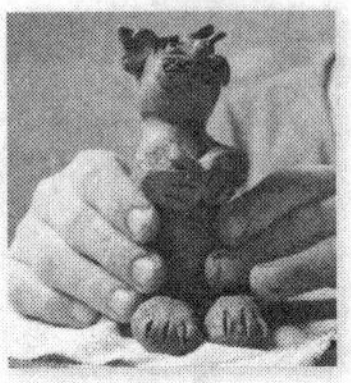 We really like ________________ our hands to make sculptures.

4 **Read and write.** Answer the questions.

1. Think of a person in your family. What activity does this person enjoy doing?

____

2. What handicrafts are you interested in doing?

____

3. What sport or game do you most enjoy playing with your friends?

____

4. What are you really good at?

____

5 **Write.** What do you enjoy doing at school? What are you interested in? What are you good at? Write three sentences.

____

____

____

Unit 6

The passive: Simple present

Rice	**is**	**grown**		in many countries.
These flowers	**are**	**found**		only in rain forests.
Corn	**is**	**eaten**	by	millions of people.
Plants	**are**	**used**	by	people as medicine.

Millions of people eat corn. = Corn ***is eaten*** *by millions of people.*
Not all sentences use *by*: *Rice* ***is grown*** *in many countries.*

1 **Read.** Circle the correct answer.

1. Nutrients **eat / are eaten** by a plant's roots.
2. The seed is **carries / carried** away by a bird.
3. Dragon blood trees are **found / find** on islands in the Indian Ocean.
4. Bees **attract / are attracted** by the pollen on some plants.

2 **Write.** Unscramble the sentences. Look at p. 98 in your Student's Book.

1. are / found / desert / the / Socotra / dragon blood trees / in / of

   Dragon blood trees are found in the desert of Socotra.

2. are / dragon blood trees / used / make / to / medicine

   ____

3. make / to / paint / trees / the / are / used / also

   ____

4. shaped / is / the / like / desert rose / an / foot / elephant's

   ____

3 **Read and write.** Complete the sentences with the correct form of the words from the box.

attract	catch	eat	~~find~~	need	pick	plant

1. Some interesting plants are found in the rain forest.
2. The rain there ________________ to help plants grow.
3. Sometimes flowers ________________ from these plants.
4. Plants ________________ by animals as well as people.
5. Insects ________________ to plants that can eat them.
6. Flies ________________ inside the Venus flytrap's leaves.

4 **Read and write.** Answer the questions.

1. What do plants need for survival?

   Light, air, water, and nutrients ________________________________

2. How does the Venus flytrap attract flies?

   ________________________________ the Venus flytrap's sweet smell.

3. Where can you find cacti plants?

   ____ in deserts.

5 **Write.** Write three sentences about what's done in your classroom each day. Use the words from the box or your own.

give	hear	make	read	see	speak	write

Homework is given by the teacher.

____

____

____

Relative clauses with *that*

I learned about a <u>plant</u>.	<u>It</u> eats insects.
I learned about a plant **that** eats insects.	
A rose is a kind of <u>flower</u>.	<u>It</u> has thorns.
A rose is a kind of flower **that** has thorns.	
The Amazon is a <u>rain forest</u>.	<u>It</u> is in South America.
The Amazon is a rain forest **that** is in South America.	
Botanists are <u>scientists</u>.	<u>They</u> study plants.
Botanists are scientists **that** study plants.	

that or *which* = things *I have a plant <u>that / which</u> kills insects.*
that or *who* = people *Botanists are scientists <u>that / who</u> study plants.*

1 **Read and write.** Complete the sentences.

1. The *Rafflesia arnoldii* is a plant that smells (smell) like rotting meat.
2. Daisies are flowers ________________ (have) yellow centers and white petals.
3. The *Hydnora africana* is a strange plant ________________ (look) like a mouth.
4. Most plants have roots ________________ (grow) under the ground.
5. The sensitive plant is a plant ________________ (move) when someone touches it.

2 **Read.** *That* is missing in five places. Write *that* where it belongs. The first one is done for you.

Meat-eating plants like the Venus flytrap are special plants ^that grow in places don't have the things most plants need for survival. For example, the soil where these plants grow may not have the nutrients needed. Such plants have found new ways to live and grow.

Like the Venus flytrap, the pitcher plant is a plant eats insects. Insects are attracted to the top of the plant, the part has the brightest colors. Then the insect is trapped by tiny hairs grow inside of the plant.

3 **Read and write.** Complete the sentences. Use *that* and information from the box.

carry / nutrients and water
climb / walls and trees
feel / sharp
have / white petals
look like / eyes
~~smell / nice~~

1. The rose is a flower that smells nice. ____________________
2. Vines are plants ____________________
3. The white baneberry has fruit ____________________
4. Daisies are flowers ____________________
5. The root is the part of the plant ____________________
6. The thorn is the part of the rose that ____________________

4 **Write.** Write five sentences to describe your favorite animals. Use *that* in your sentences.

Leopards are animals that have spots. ____________________

____

____

____

____

____

Review: Units 4–6

1 **Read.** Circle the correct answer.

1. I didn't think **anyone / no one** would buy the handicrafts that I made.

   Right, but your mom thought that someone **may / might**, didn't she?

2. Do you think **no one / anyone** will appreciate the flower garden I planted?

   Of course! **Everyone / Anyone** loves gardens! Especially gardens **that have / having** flowers.

3. Do you think **someone / everyone** else might live out in space?

   Maybe. **Finding / Find** extraterrestrials in our galaxy is something that **everyone / no one** has ever done.

2 **Read.** Circle the letter.

1. _____ is one way to pass traditions down from one generation to another.

   a. Tell stories b. Storytelling c. That tell stories

2. My aunt really enjoys _____ daisies and roses in her garden.

   a. is grown b. might grow c. growing

3. An insect that lands on a Venus flytrap _____ by the plant.

   a. might be digested b. may digest c. digesting

4. _____ can make pottery. It's not that difficult!

   a. No one b. Anyone c. Someone

5. There _____ be some new sculptures in the mueum.

   a. may b. that c. are made

6. Extraterrestrials _____ on many other planets, aren't they?

   a. find b. are found c. that find

3 Read and write.

1. Scientists study stars through a telescope. Stars are studied (by scientists) through a telescope.
2. Ancestors pass on traditions across generations. ______
3. Rocks, ice, and gas make up a comet. ______
4. The smell of rotting meat attracts insects to plants. ______

4 **Write.** Use *that* in complete sentences.

1. rose / flower / long stem

   A rose is a flower that has a long stem.
2. sunflower / flower / yellow petals

   ______
3. astronaut / person / space

   ______
4. Venus flytrap / plant / insect

   ______
5. weaving / handicraft / ancestors

   ______

5 **Write.** Complete the sentences.

1. Playing piano is my mom's favorite thing to do.
2. Reading ______
3. I enjoy ______
4. My friends are interested in ______
5. Doing homework ______

Unit 7

First conditional

If	it	**rains,**	the students	**will stay**	inside.
	the volcano	**erupts,**	we	**will leave**	our homes.

These two sentences mean the same thing. In sentence 1, notice the comma.
If it rains, the students will stay inside.
The students will stay inside if it rains.

1 **Read.** Circle the correct answer.

1. If a volcano **will erupt** / **erupts**, animals **will run** / **run** away.
2. A volcano **forms** / **will form** if magma **will push** / **pushes** up the earth's crust.
3. It **will be** / **is** difficult to breathe if gases **will blast** / **blast** into the sky.
4. If lava **will touch** / **touches** anything, it **will burn** / **burns**.

2 **Read and write.** Complete the sentences.

1. People who live near an active volcano ___won't be___ (be) safe if it erupts.
2. If scientists visit a volcano, they ________________ (collect) some ash.
3. If ash fills the air, the sky ________________ (be) blue.
4. You ________________ (see) a volcano called Mauna Loa if you go to Hawaii.

3 **Read and write.** Complete the sentences.

1. I will put on a raincoat ___if it rains___________.
2. If you plant some seeds, ________________________.
3. ________________________ if he sees a comet.
4. Lava will cover the ground ________________________.
5. If there's a tornado, ________________________.
6. ________________________ if there's a blizzard.

4 **Look and write.** Write a sentence about each picture. Use *if* and *will.*

1.  If the dog sees a cat, the dog will run toward it.

2.  ______________________________

3.  ______________________________

4.  ______________________________

5 **Write.** Write a sentence about each of the topics. Use *if* and *will* in your sentences.

extreme weather	family	hobbies
school	sports	wild animals

If I visit my grandparents this summer, we will look at old photographs.

____

____

____

____

____

____

Because of . . .

People left their homes	**because of**	the volcano.
It was hard to breathe		the ash.
We couldn't go near the crater		the heat.

You can also say: ***Because of*** *the volcano, people left their homes.* Notice the comma.

1 **Read.** Circle the letter of the logical statement in each pair.

1. a. We were in a storm shelter because of the tornado.

   b. There was a tornado because we were in a storm shelter.

2. a. Because school was canceled, there was a snowstorm.

   b. School was canceled because of a snowstorm.

3. a. Because we ran up the hill, there were big waves.

   b. We ran up the hill because of the big waves.

4. a. Because we drank lots of water, it was hot.

   b. We drank lots of water because of the heat.

2 **Unscramble.** Add commas as needed.

1. studied / the test / I / because / last night / of

   Because of the test, I studied last night. / I studied last night because of the test.

2. many / people / the / eruption / of / their / homes / because / left

   ____

3. of / because / I / the / cold / blankets / put / on

   ____

4. because / dried / up / the / drought / the / flowers / of

   ____

5. of / the / hurricane / from / the / water / the / animals / because / ran

   ____

3 **Look and write.** Complete the sentences.

1. 

Because of the music, they danced.

2. 

Because of the stop sign, ____________________

3. 

He went swimming ____________________

4. 

The plants grew ____________________

5. 

Because of the rain, ____________________

4 **Write.** Write three sentences with *because of*. Use the topics in the box or your own.

being early/late	missing school	practicing sports/music	studying

Because of my broken alarm clock, I woke up late.

____

____

____

Unit 8

Passive with modals (Simple present)

Glass	**can**		**recycled.**	
Plastic bottles	**may**	**be**	**put**	in recycling bins.
Chemicals	**must**		**used**	carefully.

may = It's OK to do something. You have permission to do it.

1 **Read.** Circle the sentence with a similar meaning.

1. The broken sink must be fixed to conserve water.
   a. Somebody has to fix the broken sink to conserve water.
   b. We can conserve water with the broken sink.
2. Green shopping bags must be used to help reduce waste.
   a. Everyone should use green shopping bags to reduce waste.
   b. We must reduce waste from green shopping bags.
3. Energy can be conserved by turning off the lights.
   a. We must always leave the lights off.
   b. We use less energy when we turn off the lights.
4. Some chemicals may be kept in special bottles.
   a. People shouldn't put some chemicals in bottles.
   b. It's possible to keep some chemicals in special bottles.

2 **Read and write.**

In order to save the environment, glass and plastic must be recycled (must / recycle). Plastic and glass bottles ________________ (can / collect) in bags. Then they ________________ (can / take) to a recycling center. These bottles also ________________ (can / reuse) in many creative ways. Plastic bottles ________________ (can / use) to make fleece jackets. Glass bottles ________________ (can / clean) with soap and water. Then they ________________ (may / fill) with water and flowers for a beautiful decoration!

3 **Write.** Use *can, must,* or *may* in your sentences.

1. plants / grow / farms

   Plants can be grown on farms.

2. trash / put / landfills

   ____

3. green bags / bring / store

   ____

4. the environment / protect

   ____

5. everything / reuse / creatively

   ____

4 **Write.** Use the words with *can, must,* or *may* to write about the objects in the photo.

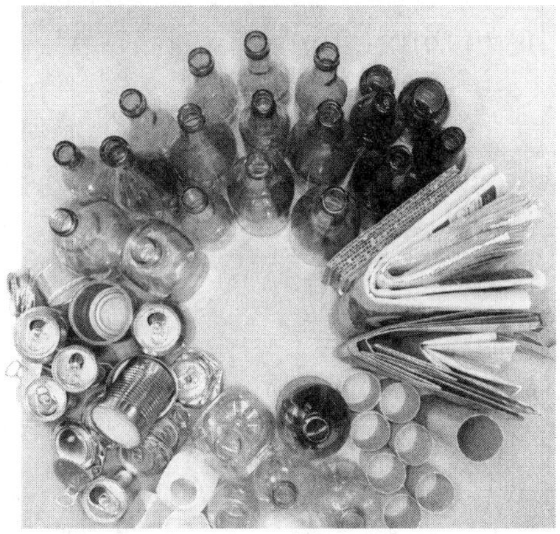

1. use Cardboard can be used to make art.
2. recycle ______________________________
3. reuse ______________________________
4. put ______________________________
5. make ______________________________

5 **Write.** Write three things that *can, must,* or *may* be done at your school to protect the environment.

We can reuse paper in our classroom.

____

____

____

Clauses with *when*

When	I leave a room,	I turn off the lights.
	she goes to school,	she walks or rides a bike.

These two sentences mean the same thing. In sentence 1, notice the comma.
When I leave a room, I turn off the lights.
I turn off the lights when I leave a room.

1 **Read.** Rewrite the sentences. Add commas if necessary.

1. We reduce our water use when we collect rainwater.

   When we collect rainwater, we reduce our water use.
2. When we reuse shopping bags, we reduce our use of plastic.

   ____
3. We reduce waste when we recycle plastic bottles.

   ____
4. When we recycle, we show that we care about the environment.

   ____

2 **Read and write.** Use phrases from the box.

make art   recycle metal   work together   ~~take long showers~~   throw away plastic

1. We waste water when we take long showers.
2. ______________________________, it sits in landfills for a long time.
3. We save energy ______________________________ instead of making new metal.
4. ______________________________ from junk, we are being creative.
5. ______________________________, we can better protect the environment.

3 **Look and write.** Complete the sentences.

1. 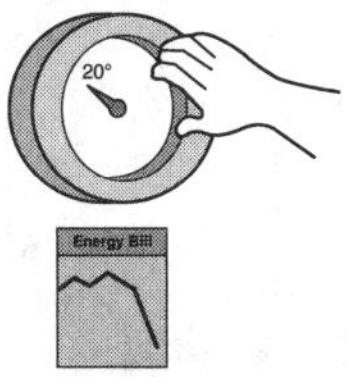

When we turn the temperature down, we conserve energy.

2. 

We are protecting the environment ______________________

____

3. 

____,

we can harm animals living in the water.

4. 

____________________________________, you can harm the environment.

4 **Write.** Complete the sentences.

1. When I am playing _______________ (sport), ______________________
2. I am happy when ______________________________________
3. When I have a test, ____________________________________
4. I get excited when _____________________________________
5. When I hear my favorite song, ____________________________

5 **Write.** How do you protect the environment? Write two sentences with *when.*

When I drink a bottle of water, I recycle the bottle.

____

____

Unit 9

Second conditional

If	I	**lived**	near mountains,	I	**would go**	hiking every weekend.	*I'd* = *I would* *he'd* = *he would*
	she	**went**	on a safari,	she	**would take**	a guide to help her.	
	I	**were**	rich,	I	**'d travel**	around the world.	
	he	**didn't have**	homework,	he	**'d go**	to the beach.	

real situation: *I don't live near mountains, so I can't go hiking every weekend.*
imagined situation: *If I **lived** near mountains, I **would go** hiking every weekend.*
With *were*: *If I/you/he/she/we/they* **were** rich . . .

1 **Read and match.** Draw a line.

1. If we stayed at a big hotel,
2. You would have so much fun
3. If I stayed at the hotel near the beach,
4. We will need passports
5. We'd go to Greece

a. if you visited a theme park.
b. I'd swim in the ocean every day.
c. if we fly to another country.
d. if my parents liked history more.
e. we would eat breakfast in its restaurant.

2 **Read and write.** Complete the sentences.

1. If they went on vacation this summer, they ___would go___ (go) somewhere on a ship.
2. They ________________ (learn) more about their ancestors if they visited their grandparents.
3. If I liked adventure, I ________________ (try) mountain climbing.
4. If they didn't love water, they ________________ (not stay) at a water park.
5. ________________ (take) photos if a tour guide showed you some ruins?

3 **Read and write.** Complete the sentences.

If I went on vacation, I ________________ (not go) to a theme park. I love history, so I'd want to go to a country with an interesting history. For example, if I ________________ (spend) time in Greece, I ________________ (be) so excited. If I ________________ (go) to Athens, I ________________ (see) all the ruins at the Acropolis. If I ________________ (have) time, I ________________ (take) pictures at all of the sites. Of course, my mom ________________ (want) to go shopping in the city if we ________________ (can). After, if we felt very tired, we ________________ (not visit) the museums. Instead, we ________________ (sit) on the beach and relax.

4 **Look and write.** Use *if* and *would* in your sentences.

1.  (see / take) If I saw lions, I'd take a picture.

2.  (play / wet) ________________________________

3.  (go camping / sleep) ________________________________

4.  (stay resort / swim) ________________________________
____

5 **Write.** Imagine your teacher is planning a class trip. Write two sentences about it using *if* and *would*.

If we went on a safari, we would learn about the animals.

____

____

Would rather

I**'d rather**	<u>play</u> outside	**than**	<u>watch</u> a movie.	*I'd = I would*
She**'d rather**	<u>go</u> swimming		(<u>go</u>) hiking.	*She'd = she would*

Question				Answer
Would you **rather**	<u>hike</u> in the forest	**or**	<u>walk</u> on the beach?	I'd rather hike in the forest.
Would he **rather**	<u>visit</u> Mexico		(<u>visit</u>) India?	He'd rather visit India.

When the verbs are the same, we don't usually say the second verb.
I'd rather <u>go</u> swimming than hiking.
Would he rather <u>visit</u> Mexico or India?

1 **Read.** Complete the sentences with *rather* and/or *than*.

1. He would ______________ fly ______________ take a boat.
2. Would they ______________ buy souvenirs ______________ see the sites?
3. I would ______________ see animals at the zoo ______________ go on safari.
4. He'd ______________ not come with us.
5. Would she ______________ go to the hotel ______________ go dancing?
6. My parents are planning a vacation, but they'd ______________ keep it a surprise.

2 **Read and write.** Complete the sentences.

1. I ___would rather swim___ in the ocean ___than (swim)___ in a lake. (swim)
2. She ______________ seafood ______________ meat. (eat)
3. ______________ get exercise on your vacation? (relax)
4. He ______________ to the beach ______________ to a water park. (go)
5. We ______________ the train ______________ the bus. (take)

3 **Write.** Ask questions with *would* and *rather*.

1. your best friend / go sightseeing / go hiking

   Would your best friend rather go sightseeing than go hiking?

2. you and your family / get a tour of the city / go shopping

   ____

3. your mother / travel by ship / fly in an airplane

   ____

4. you / visit a museum / go to the zoo

   ____

4 **Read and write.** Answer the questions in Activity 3.

1. My best friend would rather go hiking than go sightseeing.
2. ______________________________
3. ______________________________
4. ______________________________

5 **Read and write.** Your friend sent you a text message about the weekend. You don't like the activities he describes. Write a text back saying what you'd rather do.

Hi! I really want to study for math on Saturday morning. I'd also like to help my sister clean the house. Then let's go out for hamburgers. On Sunday you can come visit my grandparents with me if you'd like! Please tell me if this is OK.

I'd rather play a game than study for math.

____

____

____

____

____

____

Review: Units 7–9

1 Read. Circle the letter.

1. When we turn off the lights, ______.

   a. we conserve electricity
   b. rather than conserve electricity

2. If you stayed at this hotel, ______ in the big pool.

   a. you will swim
   b. you would swim

3. When we buy renewable materials, ______.

   a. we protect the earth
   b. we protected the earth

4. When the bottles are empty, they ______.

   a. would recycle
   b. can be recycled

5. He would rather go to the beach ______ at the water park.

   a. if he swam
   b. than swim

2 Read and write. Complete the predictions.

1. If plastic bottles go to a landfill, they ___will stay___ (stay) there for a long time.
2. If I ______________ (visit) my friends, we will talk for hours.
3. We ______________ (see) The Great Wall if we travel to China.
4. Lava will burn you if you ______________ (touch) it.
5. If my parents go on vacation, they ______________ (buy) me a souvenir.

3 Read and write. Answer the questions.

1. Should I keep the chemicals on the floor?

   no / may be No, the chemicals may be kept on a shelf.

2. Should we make some art from these old cans?

   yes / can be ______________________________

3. Should we throw away the plastic bottles?

   no / must be ______________________________

4 **Write.** Use words from each column with *if* and *would.*

I my brother/sister my parents my classmates and I	have enough money have too much homework lose electricity see a volcano erupt stay at a nice hotel visit a water park	relax in bed run very fast get wet talk to my teacher go on a safari use a flashlight swim in the pool

1. If I stayed at a nice hotel, I'd swim in the pool.
2. ______________________________
3. ______________________________
4. ______________________________

5 **Write.** Write questions. Then answer them.

1. see wildlife in a zoo / on a safari

   Question: Would you rather see wildlife in a zoo than on a safari?

   Answer: ______________________________

2. hike up a volcano / fly over a volcano

   Question: ______________________________

   Answer: ______________________________

3. go camping / stay at a resort

   Question: ______________________________

   Answer: ______________________________

6 **Write.** Use *because of* to explain three environmental problems.

Because of plastic bags, the ocean is polluted.

____

____

____

Review: Units 1–9

1 **Read.** Circle the letter.

1. The teacher said that a poisonous frog _____ as dangerous as a cobra.
   a. might be   b. would rather be   c. that is
2. Betsy _____ heard this song before.
   a. has ever   b. has never   c. have ever
3. This hotel is really beautiful, _____?
   a. is it   b. it isn't   c. isn't it
4. If I knew a volcano was active, I _____ near it.
   a. won't go   b. wouldn't go   c. go
5. If I practice the flute, I _____ in the spring concert.
   a. can be played   b. will play   c. would play
6. You don't believe that there are extraterrestials in outer space, _____?
   a. aren't there   b. don't you   c. do you

2 **Read and match.** Draw a line.

1. A rose is a flower
2. Flies are attracted to this plant
3. Instead of throwing cans away,
4. Dad thinks
5. I thought
6. When a volcano erupts,
7. If a volcano erupted near my house,
8. I really enjoy

a. the land is covered with lava and ash.
b. I would rather reuse them.
c. that has a stem with thorns.
d. there may be interesting ruins near here.
e. it would be very scary.
f. recycling old objects into art.
g. because of its sweet smell.
h. our family might go to the beach this summer.

3 **Read.** Circle the correct answer.

1. If I make some traditional food, I **will / would** share it with my friends.
2. She **will / would** stay in a resort on the beach if she went to the Caribbean.
3. We **stay / would stay** inside when we hear thunder and lightning.
4. If people recycled more, there **is / would be** less trash in landfills.

4 **Read and write.** Change the form of the words in the box.

attract
eat
paint
stay

1. ________________ safe in a storm is important.
2. The Venus flytrap is good at ________________ insects and then ________________ them.
3. ________________ is my mother's favorite hobby. She's very artistic!

5 **Write.** Rewrite the sentence.

1. Volcanoes attract many tourists to the area.

   Many tourists are attracted to the area by the volcanoes.
2. The idea of extraterrestials interests many scientists.

   ____
3. Everyone must carry umbrellas when it rains.

   ____

6 **Read and write.** Answer the questions with *going to.* Replace the underlined words.

1. Will <u>all the tourists</u> on the safari see the wildlife?

   Yes, everyone on the safari is going to see the wildlife.
2. Will <u>a member of your family</u> share stories about your past with you?

   Yes, ____
3. Will <u>any of the scientists</u> touch a poisonous frog?

   No, ____

7 **Look and write.** Make comparisons about the photos.

1.  (=, fast) ______________________________

____

2.  (+, bad) ______________________________

____

3.  (–, often) ______________________________

____

8 **Read and write.** Answer the questions in complete sentences.

1. Have you ever thrown away something important?

____

2. What would you do if you went on a safari?

____

3. Have you ever been to a jazz concert?

____

4. What would you rather do this Saturday—relax at home or go to a theme park?

____

9 **Write.** Imagine you are taking a vacation to outer space. Write a paragraph about it. Use words and phrases from the box.

as . . . as	because of	going to	if	might	would rather

____

____

____

____

GAME

Read and write. Complete each sentence. Then find the mystery message.

1. An insect is [ ][ ][ ][ ][ ][ ][ ][ ][ ] [ ][ ] the bad smell of certain plants. (1)
2. Because [ ][ ] all your practicing, you played that melody perfectly! (2)
3. Some animals have spots [ ][ ][ ][ ] [ ][ ][ ][ ][ ] their predators. (3 4)
4. If he knew how to play the guitar, we [ ][ ][ ][ ][ ] ask him to be in our band. (5)
5. We go to the beach [ ][ ][ ][ ] [ ][ ][ ][ ][ ] than I would like. I'd go every day if I could! (6 7)
6. I [ ][ ][ ][ ][ ] [ ][ ][ ][ ][ ][ ] go to the beach than to a theme park. (8)
7. [ ][ ][ ][ ][ ][ ][ ] came to see you yesterday, but I don't know who it was. (9 10)
8. Dad thought that we [ ][ ][ ][ ][ ] go to see the ruins in Greece. (11)

Mystery message:

[ ][ ][ ]['][ ][ ] [ ][ ][ ][ ][ ][ ] [ ][ ][ ][ ][ ], [ ][ ][ ][ ]['][ ] [ ][ ][ ]?

1 2 5 8 7   8 7 3 6 6 1   9 11 3 8 4   3 8 7 10 4   1 2 5